D0883190

WITHDRAWN

Earth Debates

Are Humans Damaging the Atmosphere?

Catherine Chambers

heinemann
raintree

© 2015 Heinemann Raintree
an imprint of Capstone Global Library, LLC
Chicago, Illinois

To contact Capstone Global Library, please call
800-747-4992, or visit our web site www.capstonepub.com

All rights reserved. No part of this publication may be reproduced or transmitted in any form or by any means, electronic or mechanical, including photocopying, recording, taping, or any information storage and retrieval system, without permission in writing from the publisher.

Edited by Helen Cox Cannons and Jill Kalz
Designed by Steve Mead
Original illustrations © Capstone Global Library Limited 2015
Illustrated by HL Studios, Witney, Oxon
Picture research by Tracy Cummins
Production by Helen McCreath
Originated by Capstone Global Library Limited
Printed and bound in China by CTPS

18 17 16 15 14
10 9 8 7 6 5 4 3 2 1

Library of Congress Cataloging-in-Publication Data
Chambers, Catherine, 1954-
  Is the atmosphere being damaged by humans? / Catherine Chambers.
    pages cm.—(Earth debates)
Includes bibliographical references and index.
ISBN 978-1-4846-0998-9 (hb)—ISBN 978-1-4846-1003-9 (pb)—ISBN 978-1-4846-1013-8 (ebook) 1. Atmosphere—Juvenile literature. 2. Air pollution—Juvenile literature. 3. Greenhouse effect, Atmospheric—Juvenile literature. I. Title.
  QC863.5.C427 2015
  363.739'2—dc23   2014013813

This book has been officially leveled by using the F&P Text Level Gradient™ Leveling System.

Acknowledgments
We would like to thank the following for permission to reproduce photographs: Alamy: © Arco Images GmbH, 16; Capstone: HL Studios, 4; Getty Images: AFP PHOTO, 18, Auscape/UIG, 22, Bloomberg, 37, DigitalGlobe, 15, Ivan Strba, 25, Jonathan Kingston, 9, Philippe Bourseiller, 30, SONG SANG-GI/AFP, 26, Timothy Allen, 35; NASA: Earth Observatory, 7, AIRS science team, 6, SDO, 11; Newscom: Mark & Audrey Gibson Stock Connection Worldwide, 21, ZUMA Press/Emily Stone, 8, Shutterstock: Africa Studio, 24, Alex Yeung, 32, Alison Hancock, 34, Christopher Kolaczan, 14, Claudia Otte, 12, Datskevich Aleh, 17, Franck Boston, Cover Top Right, G Tipene, 36, Gavran333, Cover Top Left, hjschneider, 27, javarman, 31, Karol Kozlowski, 13, KN, 23, kojihirano, 39, kwest, 5, leonello calvetti, Cover Middle, Mona Makela, 33, spotmatik, 41, TFoxFoto, 19, Tim Roberts Photography, 28, topten22photo, 29; SuperStock: Minden Pictures, 20.

We would like to thank Professor Daniel Block of the University of Chicago for his invaluable help in the preparation of this book.

Every effort has been made to contact copyright holders of material reproduced in this book. Any omissions will be rectified in subsequent printings if notice is given to the publisher.

All the Internet addresses (URLs) given in this book were valid at the time of going to press. However, due to the dynamic nature of the Internet, some addresses may have changed, or sites may have changed or ceased to exist since publication. While the author and publisher regret any inconvenience this may cause readers, no responsibility for any such changes can be accepted by either the author or the publisher.

Contents

Some words are shown in bold, **like this**. You can find out what they mean by looking in the glossary.

What Is the Atmosphere?

How do we decide if humans are harming our atmosphere? First, we have to find out if changes are occurring in the atmosphere. If they are, we then have to see if those changes are harmful. If they are harmful, we can try to figure out if humans are responsible and find ways to restore the atmosphere. But what is the atmosphere, and what does it do?

The atmosphere is made up of layers of gases that surround Earth. Together, these layers regulate Earth's temperature and rainfall. They also absorb or reflect rays from the Sun and protect us from burning. So, the health of the atmosphere is important to all life on Earth. If the amounts of gases within the layers change, then so do our climate conditions.

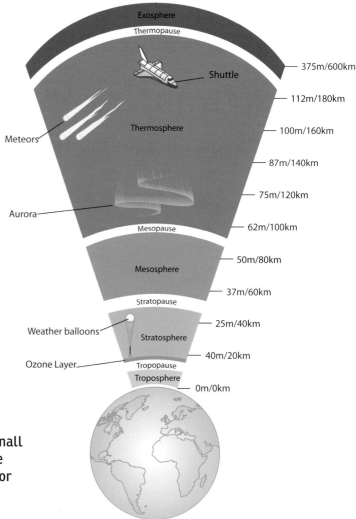

Layers of Earth's atmosphere

Exosphere

Thermopause

Shuttle — 375m/600km

— 112m/180km

Thermosphere — 100m/160km

Meteors — 87m/140km

— 75m/120km

Aurora — 62m/100km

Mesopause

— 50m/80km

Mesosphere

— 37m/60km

Stratopause

Weather balloons — 25m/40km

Stratosphere

Ozone Layer — 40m/20km

Tropopause

Troposphere — 0m/0km

>> The troposphere, stratosphere, and the thin **ozone** layer are small compared with the atmosphere as a whole. But they are vital for controlling Earth's climate.

Did you know?

Weather is the temperature and amount of rainfall, cloudiness, wind, and sunshine that we are currently experiencing. **Meteorologists** cannot predict weather for more than about a week in advance. Climate is the pattern of temperature, rainfall, cloudiness, sunshine, and wind over a long period of time. Earth's climate types vary from steamy tropical heat to freezing polar temperatures.

If you look at the diagram, you will see that the layer of gas closest to Earth is the **troposphere**. Most of our weather is made here—the winds, cloudiness, rain, hail, or snow. Thick layers of gases in the troposphere act like a blanket around Earth. These are called **greenhouse gases**, and they stop too much of the Sun's warmth from rising back through the atmosphere's layers. Examples of these gases are **carbon dioxide**, **methane**, and **nitrogen oxide**.

Without greenhouse gases, Earth would be a very chilly place. But if the layer gets too thick, it traps too much heat on Earth. It also causes the **stratosphere** (the layer above the troposphere) to cool down. Both can affect the world's climate.

⌄ Summers in Australia are becoming very hot. Is this because there is an increase in greenhouse gases?

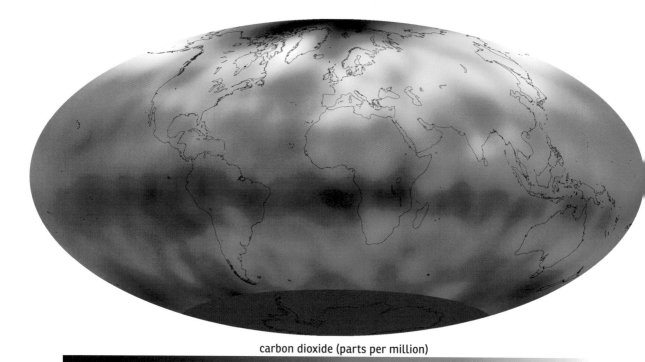

carbon dioxide (parts per million)

391   402

⌃ **NASA's** Atmospheric Infrared Sounder (AIRS), on its *Aqua* satellite, took this image of the mid-troposphere's carbon dioxide levels in May 2013. AIRS takes images day and night, and in all conditions.

How do we measure gases in the atmosphere?

Scientists have figured out that changes in the levels of two greenhouse gases in particular have the greatest effect on our climate. These gases are carbon dioxide and methane. Of these two gases, the one that concerns scientists the most is carbon dioxide. Carbon dioxide makes up just a small fraction of gases in the troposphere, yet increases in carbon dioxide levels appear to cause a lot of atmospheric changes.

Carbon dioxide is measured by scientists using two main methods. The first method uses instruments carried by atmospheric balloons or aircraft. The second method uses satellites orbiting Earth in space. These satellites carry **infrared imagers** that measure **radiation wavelengths emitted** from the atmosphere. Carbon dioxide absorbs and emits wavelengths of light that are easy to identify. They cannot be confused with any other gas, so we know the measurements are fairly accurate.

Another important gas in our atmosphere is ozone, which forms a layer that needs to be thick enough to protect Earth from the Sun's harmful rays. If you look at the diagram on page 4, you can see that the ozone layer lies just inside the stratosphere. Again, satellite imaging can measure its thickness.

The Dobson Spectrometer is a ground-based scientific instrument that measures the amount of ozone present in the atmosphere. Since the 1950s, scientists have patiently taken measurements from these instruments at ground level in the freezing Arctic and Antarctic. Their results helped discover that certain gases were destroying the ozone layer (see pages 20–21).

So, we know we can harvest information about the atmosphere and its important gases. But what have scientists discovered? Can you tell from the picture shown here?

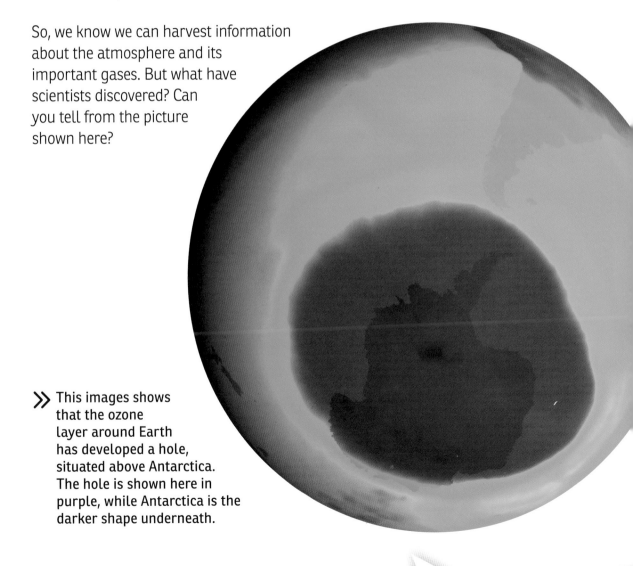

>> This images shows that the ozone layer around Earth has developed a hole, situated above Antarctica. The hole is shown here in purple, while Antarctica is the darker shape underneath.

How do we know that gas levels have changed?

The images on pages 6 and 7 only show what was happening at the time they were taken. But we can use measurements taken over the years to build a picture of changes in the atmosphere's carbon dioxide and ozone gas levels.

One very important record was made by American scientist Charles Keeling, who set up a carbon dioxide monitoring station on Hawaii's volcanic mountain of Mauna Loa. His measurements show a sharp increase in carbon dioxide levels between 1958 and 2005.

But we can study measurements even further back into prehistoric eras. Deep ice-core samples taken from Greenland and Antarctica show stripes all along their length. Each stripe represents a different time period. Bubbles of carbon dioxide gas are trapped in these bands, so we know the levels at the time when the bands formed. Results show a sharp increase in carbon dioxide levels since the beginning of the **Industrial Revolution**, over 200 years ago—and that levels are currently at their highest for at least 800,000 years. Global temperatures have also risen over this period.

The Industrial Revolution was brought about by the invention of machinery and engines that were powered by burning **fossil fuels**. Fossil fuels are made of **carbons**, and they release carbon dioxide into the atmosphere when they are burned.

These relationships prompted scientists to make links between the rise in carbon dioxide levels, global temperatures, and human activity. But there are still some scientists who do not believe that humans harm the atmosphere.

≪ Scientists have been taking ice-core samples since the 1980s.

BIOGRAPHY

Charles Keeling
(1928–2005)

American scientist Charles Keeling was one of the first climate scientists to link human activity with climate change. When he set up the Mauna Loa Observatory in Hawaii, he made sure it was far away from plants. This is because plants release carbon dioxide, and he did not want them to influence his results.

Scientists at the U.S. National Oceanic and Atmospheric Administration (NOAA) study graphs made from the data collected at Mauna Loa Observatory.

What Happens When We Burn Fossil Fuels?

How are fossil fuels made, and how much carbon dioxide do they release when they are burned? Why does this harm our atmosphere, and are humans really to blame?

We have seen that there was a sharp increase in carbon dioxide emissions during the Industrial Revolution. During this period, most engines burned coal, which releases high levels of carbon dioxide. Later, petroleum and natural gas were discovered and used as forms of energy. These, too, emit high levels of carbon dioxide. Why is this so?

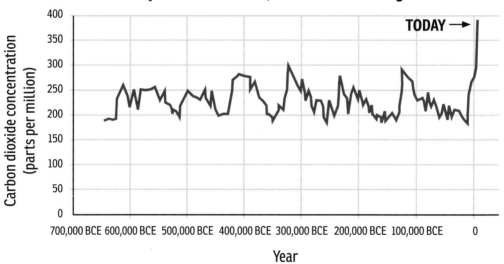

Concentration of carbon dioxide in the atmosphere from 700,000 BCE to today

⌃⌃ This graph clearly shows the sharp increase in carbon dioxide levels over the last few hundred years.

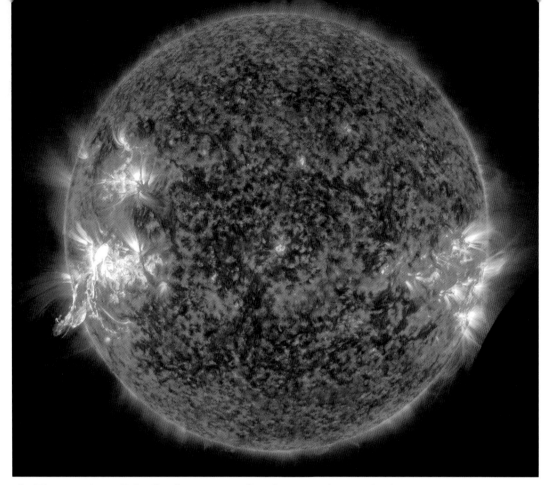

⌃ The number of the Sun's sunspots has increased over the last century. Some scientists point to this kind of solar activity as the reason for a rise in global temperatures.

Coal, petroleum oil, and natural gas are all called fossil fuels. This is because they are made from plants and creatures that lived on Earth over 300 million years ago. At that time, earthquakes, volcanoes, and shifting landmasses buried these plants and creatures after they died. Deep beneath Earth's surface, heat and pressure changed them into coal, oil, and gases. Some fossil fuels still lie deep underground, while others have been exposed to the surface.

But all fossil fuels contain a lot of carbon, because every living thing does, including us! When we burn coal, oil, and natural gas, the carbons rise into the air as carbon dioxide. So, human activity does contribute to harmful levels in gases in the atmosphere. But which activities increase levels the most?

How does creating energy affect the atmosphere?

We use energy every day—and not just when we travel. Energy brings heat, light, and air conditioning to our homes, schools, and offices. Every product we buy has required energy to manufacture, separate, or process it. Energy is also used to deal with the things we throw away! Can you think of other ways in which we use energy? Most energy sources produce gas emissions. Many of these emissions harm the atmosphere, especially carbon dioxide, methane, and nitrous oxide. But what are these energy sources?

Power plants provide our homes, schools, and factories with energy. Most of the world's power plants use coal, oil, and natural gas to make the energy. But which fuel, when burned, causes the most harm to the atmosphere?

⌄ Do we reduce sulfur dioxide levels so that the air we breathe is healthier? Or do we allow sulfur dioxide to help cool the planet?

Did you know?

Sulfur dioxide reflects sunlight, so it helps to cool the planet, but it is a heavy **pollutant**. American scientists have figured out that a coal-fired power station with no emission controls in its chimneys can emit 14,100 tons of sulfur dioxide each year. A coal plant with emission controls in the chimneys can reduce sulfur dioxide emissions to 7,000 tons. But new technology can filter some of the gases from chimneys and recycle them.

⌃ These trees have been killed by acid rain. Acid rain is made when sulfur dioxide and nitrogen oxide attach themselves to water vapor in the atmosphere.

Measurements of gas emissions show that coal fuel is the most harmful. It can produce nearly twice as much carbon dioxide as natural gas. In the United States, a single coal plant emits up to around 3.5 million tons of carbon dioxide each year. We have seen the effects of carbon dioxide on the troposphere and its links with climate change. But coal also produces nitrogen oxide, which harms the ozone layer in the stratosphere.

Coal produces harmful gases even before it is burned! Methane is emitted during mining. Methane is also a greenhouse gas, and is about 20 times more harmful in the atmosphere over a 100-year period than carbon dioxide.

⌃⌃ On some oil fields, thick, tar-like oil is mixed with sand. Extracting oil from these tar sands in Alberta, Canada, produces higher harmful gas levels than other methods of oil extraction.

How does burning oil fuel harm the atmosphere?

When oil burns in power plants, it produces the same gases as coal: carbon dioxide, sulfur dioxide, and nitrogen oxide. However, oil does emit fewer of these gases for the amount of energy produced. So, does this mean that burning oil causes less harm to the atmosphere? This is very hard to calculate. Extracting oil can use a lot of energy, depending how deep down the wells lie.

Methane leaks are one hazard of transporting oil along vast, high-pressure pipeline networks. Most oil companies **flare** the leaks on purpose. Although the dark plumes of smoke from the flares emit carbon dioxide, they are less harmful than methane emissions. But is flaring really a lasting solution?

So, what about natural gas? Natural gas was once hailed as a "clean gas" because it emits only about half the amount of carbon dioxide as coal. But natural gas extraction also leads to methane leaks.

HERO OR VILLAIN?

Is nuclear energy the answer? Nuclear power plants use **radioactive** substances such as **uranium** and **plutonium**. If these are leaked, radiation can spread quickly across oceans and continents, causing harm to all life forms.

Some scientists say that there are fewer methane emissions from the **fracking** method of gas extraction. Instead of collecting gas from large underground pockets, fracking shatters **shale** rock to release tiny pouches of the gas that are trapped inside. In the United States alone, there have been 1 million fracking sites since this technology began in the 1940s. Even small emissions from these sites really add up.

⌄ In 2011, a massive tsunami struck Japan, damaging the Daiichi nuclear power plant at Fukushima. After only 10 days, tiny particles of radiation had reached across the Pacific Ocean to California.

Does Transportation Harm the Atmosphere?

When you get into a car, train, ship, or airplane, do you think you are harming the atmosphere? All these forms of transportation burn energy and emit gases, including greenhouse gases. But which is the most harmful?

In the United States, scientists point to road transportation, which produces over 20 percent of the country's global warming emissions. It is hard to find global data on vehicle emissions. But a 2009 study showed that, on average, road travel emits 73 percent of global transportation carbon dioxide levels each year. This is a huge percentage affecting millions of people.

>> Amsterdam, in the Netherlands, has over 881,000 bicycles! In 2011, only 19.1 percent of the Netherlands' carbon dioxide emissions came from road transportation.

Did you know?

Aircraft contrail emissions can create cirrus clouds like the ones in the picture. Added to this, soot and sulfur particles in contrails can make changes within natural cirrus clouds. These changes have a warming effect.

What about aircraft? Jet aircraft, like most road transportation, use the **internal combustion engine**, which is responsible for most transportation carbon dioxide emissions. But over the last 50 years, the aircraft industry has developed **turboprop** and **turbofan** engines. These use fuel more efficiently and emit less carbon dioxide.

There are other things that produce harmful effects on our atmosphere, such as contrails. These are long, thin vapor trails, like snakes of cloud, from an aircraft's engine. Contrail emissions possibly harm the stratosphere, the layer of atmosphere above the troposphere. Here, they reduce ozone, and so increase the size of the ozone holes over the polar regions. This means that there is a reduced buffer between the Sun's burning rays and Earth.

 Neighborhood Electric Vehicles (NEVs) in busy cities run on batteries and have strict speed limits. Some vehicles run on a combination of batteries and combustion engines. These **hybrid vehicles** reduce fuel emissions.

What is the cleanest, greenest car?

Car manufacturers are responding to the concerns about harmful gas emissions. New engines that burn less fuel or emit fewer pollutants are being developed. In addition, many governments are encouraging the use of cleaner fuels such as **biofuels** that are made from plants.

Some environmentalists believe that electric cars are the cleanest. These cars run on batteries rather than internal combustion engines. But batteries need to be charged, which uses energy burned in power stations!

> "The global warming potential from electric vehicle production is about twice that of conventional vehicles... If you are considering purchasing an electric vehicle for its environmental benefits, first check your electricity source."

Professor Anders Hammer Stromman, from a study by the Norwegian University of Science and Technology, 2012

In addition to this, the process of manufacturing an electric car uses up more energy, which also comes from power stations. So, the **carbon footprint** of an electric car can be even larger than that of a car that uses gasoline or diesel fuel.

Is this true for all electric cars and their batteries? It depends on the source of the electricity used to manufacture them. If the energy comes from coal-fired or heavy-oil power stations, then a lot of greenhouse gases will be emitted. But if a mix of fuel sources has been used, including nuclear power or natural gas, then electric vehicles are less harmful to the atmosphere. How do we know if an electric car has been manufactured using energy that is less harmful? Generally, the fuel source used to make electricity depends on the country you live in, but can be very hard to know. For the moment, there are no answers.

⌄ Batteries contain many **toxic** substances. When they are broken down and burned, they emit gases such as sulfur dioxide.

Do Aerosols Damage the Atmosphere?

What happens when we squirt foam or a liquid from an aerosol spray can? Do we think of the gases released at the same time? It has been proven that these gases have affected levels of ozone. So, let's remind ourselves what ozone is and what it does.

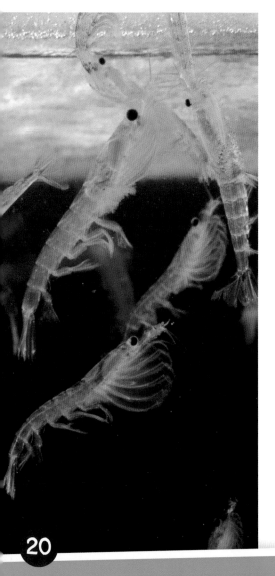

Ozone is a very rare and important gas in our atmosphere, and the ozone layer takes up very little space within it. The layer begins at between 6 and 10 miles (10 and 17 kilometers) above Earth's surface, and only reaches about 32 miles (50 kilometers) at its thickest point. Yet, in spite of its slenderness, the ozone layer plays a vital role in the stratosphere. Here, the ozone molecules absorb most of the Sun's ultraviolet (UV-B) rays. This stops them from reaching Earth, where they can burn skin and plants, causing damage and disease. The ozone layer also keeps the stratosphere at a constant, warm temperature.

« These Antarctic krill are tiny, shrimp-like creatures that are food for many of the Southern Ocean's fish, mammals, and birds. During the Antarctic's spring, from September to November, the ozone layer above the Antarctic is at its thinnest. But krill have a defense against the Sun's burning UV rays. They eat plenty of plant-like algae, which contain a chemical sunscreen.

Over 30 years ago, no one had any reason to suspect that aerosol gases were harming the atmosphere. But in the early 1980s, Professor Joseph Farman, a British physicist, discovered that ozone levels above Antarctica had become so low that there was a hole in the layer. NASA satellite data confirmed his findings. Scientific laboratory tests had already discovered that chlorofluorocarbon (CFC) gas emissions from aerosols could destroy ozone. So, the link was made between CFCs and the depletion of ozone gases in the stratosphere.

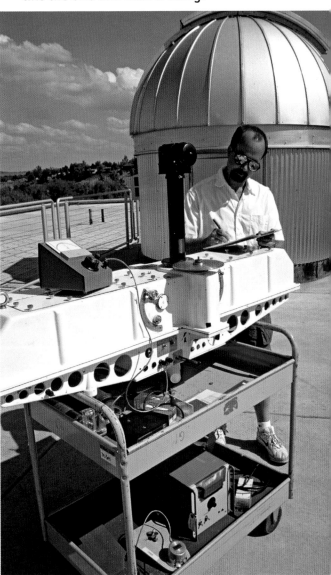

⌄ Professor Joseph Farman had measured levels on the ground since 1956, using Dobson Spectrometers like the one this man is using.

BIOGRAPHY

Susan Solomon (born 1956)

Susan Solomon is a professor of atmospheric chemistry and climate science. Back in the mid-1980s, she figured out how CFC emissions reduce ozone over the poles. She discovered that CFCs react with ozone on tiny ice particles in stratospheric clouds. Later, she showed that, in warmer parts of the world, volcanic activity can add to a similar decrease in ozone levels.

⌃ Australia's Great Barrier Reef is made up of nearly 2,500 different coral reefs and 400 species. But the corals you see here died from overexposure to sunlight due to a thin ozone layer.

Have we restored ozone levels?

After 1985, scientists discovered that stratospheric ozone levels had decreased all over the world, not just at the poles. So, the problem was huge. Ozone levels go up and down each year, but the trend is now upward. This is because the world responded to the problem.

In 1987, 28 nations were represented at a meeting in Montreal, Canada, to find a way to reduce CFC emissions. As a result, 46 countries signed a treaty called the Montreal Protocol, which pledged to cut emissions of widely used CFCs by 50 percent by December 1999. Since then, they have renewed their promise. NASA scientists predict that ozone levels will be restored to levels that will protect Earth from the Sun's burning rays by 2070.

How will this happen? Manufacturers have been forced to remove CFCs from aerosols, refrigerators, air-conditioning systems, fire-suppressants, solvents such as cleaning agents, and other products. They have replaced ozone-**depleting** substances (ODS) with other chemicals. Has this been successful?

By 2011, the United States had replaced 84 percent of its ODS, mostly with **hydrofluorocarbons (HFCs)**. But this has led to another threat to the health of the atmosphere. Some HFCs are greenhouse gases that affect the troposphere and contribute to climate change. They have some impact on ozone, too. Now, scientists are identifying the worst HFCs, and these are being phased out.

Eyewitness

Parwan Bhartia was feeling the pressure. Since 1977, this NASA atmospheric scientist had been instructed to find out if CFCs on Earth were destroying the ozone layer. Could the new *Nimbus-7* satellite help provide answers? By 1981, there were small hints that ozone was reducing slightly. Then, bang! In 1984, the data showed a huge hole in the ozone layer.

⌄ Many of us still use a lot of old products that contain CFCs and other ODS. Many lie in waste dumps around the world.

Do Plastics Harm the Atmosphere?

What would we do without plastics? Plastics are easily molded to any shape. They can be soft or rigid, thick or thin. Plastics are easy to keep clean. For all these reasons, we use plastics in many products, from cell phone cases and plastic bags to furniture and tiny, life-saving surgical devices. How many plastic items can you see around you right now? Plastics are so useful that we may be ignoring their harm to the atmosphere.

Where does the link between plastics on Earth and atmospheric gases begin? The main material in plastics comes from **petrochemicals**, which are based on oil. As we saw on pages 14 and 15, oil is a fossil fuel that can create greenhouse gases that harm the troposphere.

⋁ Designers enjoy the shapes, colors, and textures that plastics can give.

⌃ Plastics can be used to insulate the walls of buildings.

Scientists have calculated that across the world, plastics use only about 4 percent of petrochemicals annually. But another 4 percent is added during extraction and manufacturing. They have also figured out that plastics production is increasing by about 9 percent every year. So, the problem for our atmosphere is escalating.

One of the biggest plastic hazards is polystyrene. This lightweight foam is incredibly useful. For example, it is used to insulate buildings so that we can keep heat in during the winter, and heat out during the summer. This helps to reduce our use of heating and air-conditioning, and therefore emissions of greenhouse gases. Polystyrene is also used to protect goods from being damaged during transportation.

However, most polystyrene is made of hydrofluorocarbons (HFCs). As we saw on page 23, certain HFCs create greenhouse gases and have some impact on the ozone layer in the stratosphere. So, we know that making plastics affects our atmosphere. But what happens when we throw them away?

What's the harm when plastics break down?

Plastic waste is scattered in dumps and buried in landfill sites across the world. Plastic litter scars our landscapes and pollutes our oceans. It is estimated that about 10 percent of the world's waste is made of plastics. But how does this affect the atmosphere? Plastics in dumps and landfill sites are often burned to dispose of them. This contributes to the 100 million tons of carbon gases emitted by making and destroying plastics.

> **Landfill capture of methane is not 100 percent efficient, nor does it begin immediately after the material is put into the landfill. Therefore, there will be emissions from biodegradation that will reach the atmosphere. It is important to be aware of how accelerating the production of methane would change overall emissions.**

Professor Matthew Realff, School of Chemical and Biomolecular Engineering, Georgia Institute of Technology

So, what are the alternatives? Plastics take hundreds of years to break down—some say thousands of years! As a result, scientists are trying to find ways to speed up the process. They are developing plastic materials that include bacteria and fungi to make them more **biodegradable**, which means that they will break down more easily into natural substances. Scientists are confident that some of these new plastics will biodegrade within 5 to 10 years.

But there are problems. The first is that this new technology does not yet apply to all plastics. The second is that the material releases methane gas as it biodegrades. Methane gas is more harmful to the atmosphere than the same amount of carbon dioxide from burned plastics. However, methane capture on landfill sites is also being developed. This methane can be flared or reused as fuel.

⌄ This switchgrass can be made into biodegradable plastics! Other grasses, rice, and potatoes can also be used. But they all emit methane when they break down.

Does Farming Harm the Atmosphere?

What happens to food before it reaches our plate? Every stage of food production has an impact on the atmosphere. The United Nations Food and Agricultural Organization reported that between 2000 and 2010, greenhouse gas emissions from agriculture grew by 1.6 percent every year. By 2010, 5 billion tons were reaching the troposphere annually.

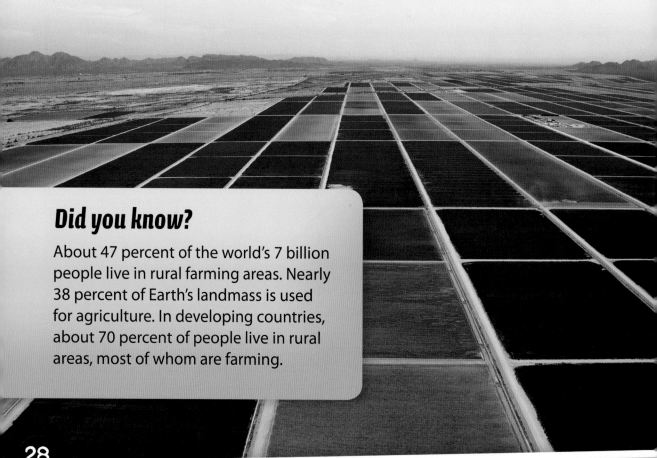

Did you know?

About 47 percent of the world's 7 billion people live in rural farming areas. Nearly 38 percent of Earth's landmass is used for agriculture. In developing countries, about 70 percent of people live in rural areas, most of whom are farming.

⌃ All these fruits and vegetables are part of a traditional food culture. So, it is hard to ask people to change what they eat or the way they grow their crops.

The harm begins on the land where food crops are grown and livestock are reared. Food crops include wheat, oats, rice, vegetables, and fruits, which most of us eat every day. We need a lot of land to provide enough food crops for the world's growing population. Often forests and other natural habitats have to be cleared to make way for agriculture.

Many of these natural habitats are **carbon sinks**—so called because the plants growing in them absorb a lot of carbon dioxide gas and prevent it from reaching the troposphere. Sometimes natural vegetation is burned to make way for agriculture. This destroys a carbon sink and at the same time releases harmful carbon dioxide from the burning plant matter. Of course, crops are also plant matter and absorb carbon dioxide, but not as much as ecosystems such as rain forests. So, even before any seed is sown, agriculture harms the atmosphere by removing effective carbon sinks.

However, should we really blame farming when natural processes, such as wildfires, also destroy natural habitats? These fires release vast amounts of greenhouse gases into the atmosphere.

What are agrochemicals, and what do they do to the atmosphere?

Farmers are growing three times more crops than they were in the 1960s. Often a higher crop yield, or amount, is grown on the same piece of land that was used 50 years ago. How can the farmer produce a higher yield in the same space?

To achieve these yields, most farmers use agrochemicals. These are chemicals that will help ensure a healthy, heavy crop. First, they apply chemical fertilizers, which help crops to grow. But chemical fertilizers contain nitrates, which emit nitrous oxide. This greenhouse gas can warm the atmosphere 300 times more than carbon dioxide.

⌄ In dry parts of the world, grazing animals can reduce the land to dust and remove carbon-releasing plants.

⌃ Rice plants decay in water, where they are starved of oxygen.

Once the crops have started to grow, farmers then use chemical **pesticides** and **herbicides** to get rid of insect pests and weeds. **Fungicides** prevent molds from destroying the crop. Many of these chemicals reach the atmosphere, including **organochlorine** pesticides that can deplete the ozone layer. They can also stay in the soil and air for many years. In recent years, some of the most harmful agrochemicals have been banned.

However, the biggest problem is methane gas. Huge amounts of methane are emitted from decaying plant matter in wet rice fields and from the stomachs of plant-eating livestock such as cattle, sheep, and goats.

HERO OR VILLAIN?

We blame farming for harming the atmosphere, but there are no easy solutions. Around 842 million people worldwide currently do not have enough to eat, so we badly need food crops. In places where it is difficult to grow crops, people raise livestock for food and to sell. What should we do about methane emissions from rice? Is there an acceptable alternative for the world's 3 billion people who eat rice as a main part of their diet?

How Do Buildings Harm the Atmosphere?

It may be hard to see how buildings can harm the atmosphere. For example, they do not decompose to release methane. However, the construction, operation, and maintenance of buildings have a big impact on the environment. There are many stages in building, from the making or extracting of building materials to transporting them to the building site. Each stage has an effect on the atmosphere.

Did you know?

Global building is responsible for:

- 30–40% of global energy consumption
- 30% of greenhouse gas emissions
- over 3 billion tons of raw materials used annually
- 20% of global water usage

Green buildings can deliver:

- 30–50% reduction in energy use
- 35% decrease in carbon emissions
- 70% decrease in waste output
- 40% reduction in water usage

Source: United Nations Environment Programme (UNEP) 2012

⋀ This building in New Mexico is being constructed from recycled materials such as car tires. Recycling means fewer greenhouse gas emissions. But in this remote area, how many were emitted through transporting the materials?

In the United States, 25 percent of all greenhouse gas emissions come from buildings. This figure does not include emissions from clearing land before construction begins. In the United Kingdom, an amazing 50 percent of all fossil-fuel energy is used to construct buildings and to keep them heated or cooled and lit.

Where does the harm to the atmosphere begin? It starts with land clearance that uses heavy machinery and a lot of fossil fuels. Land clearance also destroys the trees and plants that absorb carbon dioxide. Land surface that is covered by buildings, roads, or parking lots can no longer soak up rainwater. Instead, the water evaporates in the sunshine, carrying polluting chemicals (especially from vehicles) up into the atmosphere.

Which building materials harm the atmosphere most?

Concrete is a very useful building material. It is poured into the ground to make strong foundations. It can be molded into blocks, pillars, and beams to create everything from sheds to sky-scraping office buildings. But concrete and the cement that binds bricks and blocks together use materials and energy that add masses of greenhouse gases to the atmosphere.

The main ingredient of concrete is limestone, which is quarried from the ground. When it is heated with clay-like materials to make cement, the kiln temperature can reach 2,552 degrees Fahrenheit (1,400 degrees Celsius). Processing limestone uses a lot of fossil-fuel energy, and it produces 5 percent of the world's carbon dioxide emissions.

⌄ Concrete does not always last. Water and chemicals seep into tiny cracks and make the concrete crumble.

Eyewitness

"It is the dry season here in Mali, West Africa. I am staring in awe at the Great Mosque of Djenne, the world's biggest sun-baked brick building. It was designed by a stonemason, Ismaila Traore, in 1907. With its palm-tree trunk supports and sun-baked brick structure, the mosque does little harm to our atmosphere. But in the rainy season, the torrential storms wash away the plaster. That's why today, the people of Djenne are taking part in the annual replastering festival!"

Using a report from David Rich, a travel writer for GoNOMAD

Buildings made of bricks are also harmful to the environment. In some parts of the world, baking clay bricks is a small-scale industry. It often takes place in rural areas that have good supplies of clay but poor supplies of sustainable energy. Trees that are cut down for wood to fuel the brick-making kilns are often not replaced. Firing the kilns produces high levels of carbon emissions—and cutting down trees reduces carbon sinks. However, fire-baked brick buildings can last for hundreds of years, so harm to the atmosphere is greatly reduced over their lifetime.

What about waste?

The building industry creates a huge amount of waste through the over-ordering of building materials, storing them badly so that they decay, or damaging them. Transporting these unused building materials produces unnecessary gas emissions. Figures show that about 440 million tons of materials are delivered to the world's building sites each year. But 66 million tons of this go to waste!

Transporting heavy building materials contributes to the harm to the atmosphere. In addition to emitting greenhouse gases, heavy trucks damage roads, which then need to be repaired. Building and repairing roads uses yet more fossil fuels.

So, how is the building industry trying to reduce the damage? First, more architects are designing buildings made from renewable and long-lasting materials. These include wood that can be replaced by planting trees in sustainable forests. New technology is improving the manufacture of concrete and bricks. Modern kilns can now capture and reuse burned fuels, which reduces gas emissions.

˅ Architects in the city of Sydney, Australia, now design with the health of the planet in mind. The "Sustainable Sydney Walking Tour" shows the city's best examples of "green" design and construction.

There is growing interest in the use of traditional building materials that only need to be extracted and transported, not manufactured. These materials include flint, stone, and bricks that do not need to be fired in a kiln. These bricks are made from clay bound together with horsehair and dried in the Sun.

BIOGRAPHY

Norman Foster, architect (born 1935)
You cannot miss Norman Foster's award-winning buildings! They include the stunning shapes and shiny surfaces of his wing at the Museum of Fine Arts, Boston, and China's Beijing Airport. But Foster understands the importance of cutting down on greenhouse gases. He and his team are currently designing Masdar, a whole new city in Abu Dhabi, and they are aiming for zero-carbon emissions and zero waste.

Can Humans Help the Atmosphere?

So, why should we care about the atmosphere? The atmosphere protects us and provides the air we breathe. Clouds form in our atmosphere and bring the rain that waters our crops. Carbon sinks that soak up extra greenhouse gases are not large enough to take all the harmful gases in the atmosphere. Our oceans, Earth's biggest carbon sinks, are already absorbing so much carbon dioxide that some marine life is suffering. How can humans help?

> " **Preventing global warming from becoming a planetary catastrophe may take something even more drastic than renewable energy, super-efficient urban design, and global carbon taxes.** "
>
> Jamais Cascio, Institute for the Future, California

Scientists are finding solutions to some of the most difficult problems, such as gas emissions from power plants. They have developed **Carbon Capture and Storage** (CCS) technologies to trap and contain escaping gases. However, CCS installations are expensive.

In the United Kingdom, the new White Rose CCS project is planning a new type of power plant that will capture 90 percent of all gas emissions. The emissions will then be transported by pipeline deep beneath the bed of the North Sea. Here, they will be stored. Will they be safe? Time will tell. The plant will burn coal, the most harmful fossil fuel. But it will also burn **biomass**, which is natural plant waste.

This brings us to another innovation to help the atmosphere—the use of renewable biofuels for transportation. Biofuels can include biomass, but most are made from crops such as corn and palm oil. However, a lot of natural vegetation is being destroyed in order to grow them. As we saw on pages 28 and 29, this removes valuable carbon sinks. There are no easy ways to help the atmosphere.

⌄ Wind, solar, and wave power are all alternative ways to create energy. They do not emit gases, but making the equipment and transporting it does!

Are Humans Really Harming the Atmosphere?

The levels of gases in Earth's atmosphere have changed. This is something that scientists can now measure. But are humans responsible? If we are, have we upset the atmosphere so much that we have caused our climate to change as well? And is this causing more dramatic weather events, such as hurricanes, floods, droughts, and blizzards?

The temperature of Earth's surface has risen and fallen throughout time. It seems that sunspots and flares might cause slow changes. Scientists believe that Earth's orbit closer to the Sun also affects our climate. Certain natural conditions can trigger extreme weather events. These include the sudden warming or cooling of the tropical Pacific Ocean.

But do any of these factors explain why Earth's atmosphere has warmed by almost 1.8 degrees Fahrenheit (1 degree Celsius) since the beginning of the Industrial Revolution 200 years ago?

> " In the next century it's definitely going to get warmer... You don't need a crystal ball or fancy climate model to say that. Just look at the sea level and temperature records from the past 100 years—they're all going up. Unlike people, the climate has a very long memory. "

Josh Willis, climate scientist at NASA's Jet Propulsion Laboratory

What can we do to help the atmosphere? We can recycle our waste so that it does not end up making methane gases in landfill sites. We can walk, cycle, or take the bus rather than ride in a car. We can remember to switch off our computers and lights when we are not using them. This will reduce our bills, too!

Climate skeptics point to periods within the last 200 years when Earth's temperature cooled for a while. But these cool periods have not dipped to the lowest levels measured before we started pumping gases into the atmosphere in a big way.

Many scientists firmly believe in the link between gases that humans have released into the atmosphere and changes in our climate. For them, the answer is, "Yes, humans have harmed the atmosphere." What do YOU think?

Quiz

How much do you remember about the atmosphere from reading this book? You could find out by answering these questions. You can use the index to help you. Some of the answers might lie in the boxes and captions as well as the main text.

1 Which layer of the atmosphere holds the most greenhouse gases?

   A mesosphere
   B stratosphere
   C troposphere
   D exosphere

2 Which one of these gases is not a greenhouse gas?

   A methane
   B oxygen
   C carbon dioxide
   D nitrogen oxide

3 Burning fossil fuels affects the atmosphere. Which one of these is not a fossil fuel?

   A coal
   B ethanol
   C petroleum oil
   D natural gas

4 Which type of engine is most harmful to the atmosphere?

   A turboprop
   B internal combustion
   C turbofan
   D electric motor

5 What effect do chlorofluorocarbons (CFCs) found in aerosol sprays and refrigerators have on the atmosphere?

   A They add to greenhouse gases.
   B They cause acid rain.
   C They thin the protective ozone layer around Earth.
   D They thicken the protective ozone layer around Earth.

6 Plastics are harmful to the atmosphere. Which one of these statements about the harm they do is false?

A Plastics do not biodegrade easily.

B Plastics cannot be easily cleaned and so attract pollutants.

C Plastics emit carbon dioxide, a greenhouse gas, when they are burned.

D Polystyrene plastic foam is made of harmful hydrofluoro-carbons (HFCs) that can create greenhouse gases.

7 Which greenhouse gas is emitted from the stomachs of cattle and other plant-eating livestock?

A sulfur dioxide

B carbon dioxide

C nitrous oxide

D methane

8 What makes fired brick less harmful than many other building materials?

A Fired brick can be broken up and used in construction.

B Fired brick is heated at very high temperatures.

C Fired brick can last for hundreds of years, reducing harm to the atmosphere over its lifetime.

D Fired brick is biodegradable.

9 Which of these natural events releases harmful amounts of sulfur gases into the air?

A earthquake

B lightning storm

C wild forest fire

D volcano

10 Which one of these actions that we can do will NOT help the atmosphere?

A Recycling our waste can help the atmosphere.

B Throwing our waste away so it ends up in just one place (for example, a landfill site) can help the atmosphere.

C Walking or cycling can help the atmosphere.

D Turning off lights and computers when we do not need them can help the atmosphere.

ANSWERS: 1C, 2B, 3B, 4B, 5C, 6B, 7D, 8C, 9D, 10B

Glossary

biodegradable material, mostly plant and animal, that can be broken down easily

biofuel renewable fuel made from plant matter

biomass fuel created using plant and animal matter

carbon chemical element found in coal, oil, and other substances. When they are burned, they release the carbon as a gas, such as carbon dioxide.

Carbon Capture and Storage (CCS) capturing carbon dioxide from power plants or factory chimneys, then transporting and burying it so it is not released into the atmosphere

carbon dioxide greenhouse gas released by burning fossil fuels; also one of several impure gases removed from natural gas fuel before it is used

carbon footprint calculated amount of carbon dioxide it takes to make a product, go on a car journey, recycle waste, and all other activities

carbon sink place on Earth where carbon dioxide from the atmosphere is absorbed. Examples are tropical rain forests and the ocean.

deplete reduce

emit throw out or up into the air

flare burn off emissions of gas or oil

fossil fuel fuel made from living things millions of years ago. When burned, it releases greenhouse gases.

fracking fracturing rock using high-pressure jets of water to release natural gas from within the rock

fungicide chemical used to destroy molds and fungi

greenhouse gas gas that causes climate change, particularly global warming

herbicide chemical used to destroy unwanted plants (weeds)

hybrid vehicle vehicle that is powered both by fuel and electric battery

hydrofluorocarbon (HFC) chemical compound used as a coolant in refrigerators, air-conditioning units, and products such as polymer foams

Industrial Revolution period from the late 18th century to mid-19th century when inventions in industrial processes led to a huge increase in manufacturing and burning of fossil fuels

infrared imager instrument that can measure heat by detecting the amount of radiation emitted by an object, piece of land, and so on

internal combustion engine engine in which the expansion of fuel and oxygen in a chamber push against moving parts, making a vehicle or machine move

meteorologist scientist who studies the atmosphere

methane greenhouse gas released by burning fossil fuels

NASA National Aeronautical and Space Administration, where research into space and aeronautics takes place

nitrogen oxide greenhouse gas released by burning fossil fuels

organochlorine toxic chemical used in pesticides and other products

ozone gas type that forms a layer in the stratosphere that protects Earth from the Sun's harmful rays

pesticide toxic chemical substance that is used to control insect pests on crops and other plants

petrochemical chemical product made from petroleum oil and sometimes coal or gas

plutonium radioactive substance used to make fuel in a nuclear power station

pollutant substance, gas, or chemical that is harmful or poisonous

radiation wavelength wavelength radiated from the Sun, such as ultraviolet light, radio waves, and infrared waves

radioactive substance used in nuclear fuels that can create harmful rays if leaked

shale fine-grained, flaky type of rock

stratosphere layer of Earth's atmosphere above the troposphere

sulfur dioxide gas that is harmful to human health and is produced by burning coal

toxic harmful or poisonous

troposphere first layer of Earth's atmosphere

turbofan aircraft engine type that uses a propeller-type fan with the engine's jet component to reduce fuel consumption and engine noise

turboprop aircraft engine that reuses the exhaust to help move the propeller, so it reduces exhaust fumes and reduces fuel consumption

uranium radioactive chemical element used in creating nuclear fuels

Find Out More

If you want to find out more about the atmosphere, take a look at some of these books and web sites. In addition to this, you could take part in any school activity or club that helps clean up your environment and reuses any waste you collect. You could also try to reduce the waste in your home.

Books

Hartman, Eve, and Wendy Meshbesher. *Climate Change* (Sci-Hi). Chicago: Raintree, 2010.

Hunter, Rebecca. *Climate Change* (Eco Alert). Mankato, Minn.: Sea-to-Sea, 2012.

Morgan, Sally. *Global Warming* (Science at the Edge). Chicago: Heinemann Library, 2009.

Web Sites

FactHound offers a safe, fun way to find Internet sites related to this book. All of the sites on FactHound have been researched by our staff.

Here's all you do:

Visit www.facthound.com

Type in this code: 9781484609989

Places to Visit

Local and national science and technology museums often feature exhibitions about the atmosphere, the environment, and climate change. For example, you can check out the following:

The Exploratorium, San Francisco, California
www.exploratorium.edu

The Exploratorium is a science museum with hands-on exhibits that encourage visitors to directly engage with science. Among its many fascinating exhibits is the Bay Observatory Gallery, which explores the surrounding San Francisco Bay area, including its ecology and weather patterns.

Museum of Science, Boston, Massachusetts
www.mos.org

The Museum of Science, Boston, features many exhibits that explore issues relating to the atmosphere and problems affecting Earth. Check out "Catching the Wind," which explores the use of turbines and wind energy. "Conserve @ Home" shows you how you might be wasting energy in your home. "Energized!" explores natural energy sources such as the Sun, water, and wind. Finally, "WeatherWise" explains the science of meteorology.

The Museum of Science and Industry, Chicago, Illinois
www.msichicago.org

Here, you can explore the "Future Energy Chicago" exhibition. This begins with an explanation of different forms of energy and then allows visitors to compete to find the most environmentally friendly solutions to problems such as transportation, car design, and home design. "Earth Revealed" investigates different issues affecting our planet, including climate and weather. The museum also features many revolving exhibits about climate and the environment.

Index